When I am afraid, I put my trust in you.
Psalm 56:3 (NIV)

Do not fear, for I am with you...
Isaiah 41:10 (NIV)

To Mommy and Dad
who taught me where my hope comes from

www.buildfaithco.com

I MAY BE WEAK BUT HE MAKES ME STRONG

Written by JoAnne John

Illustrated by Samira John

God has an amazing
plan for you,
Even when you don't
know what to do.

When in doubt,
or on a hard day,
Sing this song
to help you on your way:
"I may be weak
but He makes me strong.
He walks with me
all the day long."

As you grow older,

life can get tough.

Some people aren't kind

and some can be rough.

On those days,

we try to understand.

Are these hard lessons

part of God's plan?

Even on a rainy and cloudy day,

God will still help you on your way.

You -- yes you! --
can do hard things,
Even with the
troubles that life brings.

Never give up and
have faith in who you are.
Trust in the Lord
and you will go far.

Dream big,

dream in full colors.

You are unique.

You were never meant

to be like others.

Smile bright and

follow His way.

Make time to read

God's Word every day.

But when in doubt,
or on a hard day,
Sing this song
to help you
on your way:

"I may be weak
but He makes me strong.
He walks with me
all the day long."

#1
SCIENCE FAIR

Never forget,
the Lord will be with you.
His boundless love
will see you through.

Science, English,
math, geography,
Art, dance
sports, and history.

God gave you a mind
to discover great things.
You are a WONDERFUL
human being!

fresh
PRODUCE

With each challenge,
you will grow.
The more you experience,
the more you know.

Flowers, plants,
and trees grow too.
God created many things
just for you.

VELOCITY
SPHERE
ASTRO
MATH
PATTERSON
HOLY SPIRIT
READING

Joy and light are what
He wants us to be.
Even on days
when it's not clear to see.

You will learn to be

courageous and overcome.

Because God is where our

hope comes from.

But when in doubt,
or on a hard day,
Sing this song
to help you
on your way:

"I may be weak
but He makes me strong.
He walks with me
all the day long."

Pray, and don't
give up the fight.
God will protect you
with all His might.
When life is a mess,
He will be with you.
Just do your best --
it's all we can do.

50¢
Lemonade

When you are afraid and your eye sheds a tear,
Remember that God says, "Do not fear."

Use your great mind to change the world,
In the hearts of every boy and girl.

Will you prevail?
Will you figure it out?
Yes, indeed,
there is no doubt!
Pray and seek
His amazing love.
Watch as the blessings
pour down from above.
You are smart, loving, and,
most of all, kind.
Focus on God.
Leave your worries behind.

But when in doubt,
or on a hard day,
Sing this song
to help you on your way:

"I may be weak
but He makes me strong.
He walks with me
all the day long."

JoAnne John is a first-time author, mother to Samira and Micah, and wife to Robby . She is passionate about encouraging children to keep their faith and pursue their dreams. This book was inspired by a poem she wrote her daughter as she transitioned from tween to teenager, hoping she would be reminded of God's love for her, especially on those hard days.

Samira John is a first-time illustrator and lover of all things crafty and pretty. She has always been passionate about art, design, and beautifying things. She illustrated these images at age 13 to support her mom's dream of creating a children's book and to learn more about graphic design. Her family loves her tremendously and are extremely proud of her.

When I am afraid, I put my trust in you.
Psalm 56:3 (NIV)

Do not fear, for I am with you...
Isaiah 41:10 (NIV)

* 9 7 9 8 8 6 9 1 0 9 0 8 8 *